ANNIE BAKER

Annie Baker's other plays at the National include *The Antipodes* (also at the Signature Theatre); *John* (also at the Signature Theatre, Obie Award, Evening Standard Award nomination) and *The Flick* (also at Barrow Street; Pulitzer Prize for Drama, Hull-Warriner Award, Susan Smith Blackburn Award, Obie Award, Evening Standard Award, and Olivier nomination). She's the author of *Circle Mirror Transformation* (Obie Award and Drama Desk nomination for Best New American Play) at Playwrights Horizons and the Royal Court; *The Aliens* (Obie Award) at Rattlestick Playwrights Theater and the Bush; and an adaptation of Chekhov's *Uncle Vanya* at Soho Rep (Drama Desk nomination for Best Revival), for which she also designed the costumes. Her plays have been produced at over 150 theatres throughout the US and in more than a dozen other countries. Other recent honours include a MacArthur Fellowship, Guggenheim Fellowship, Steinberg Playwriting Award, American Academy of Arts and Letters Award and the Cullman Fellowship at the New York Public Library.

Other Titles in this Series

Annie Baker
THE ANTIPODES
THE FLICK
JOHN

Chris Bush
THE ASSASSINATION OF KATIE HOPKINS
THE CHANGING ROOM
A DREAM
FAUSTUS: THAT DAMNED WOMAN
HUNGRY
JANE EYRE *after* Brontë
THE LAST NOËL
ROCK/PAPER/SCISSORS
STANDING AT THE SKY'S EDGE
    with Richard Hawley
STEEL

Jez Butterworth
THE FERRYMAN
JERUSALEM
JEZ BUTTERWORTH PLAYS: ONE
JEZ BUTTERWORTH PLAYS: TWO
MOJO
THE NIGHT HERON
PARLOUR SONG
THE RIVER
THE WINTERLING

Caryl Churchill
BLUE HEART
CHURCHILL PLAYS: THREE
CHURCHILL PLAYS: FOUR
CHURCHILL PLAYS: FIVE
CHURCHILL: SHORTS
CLOUD NINE
DING DONG THE WICKED
A DREAM PLAY *after* Strindberg
DRUNK ENOUGH TO SAY I LOVE YOU?
ESCAPED ALONE
FAR AWAY
GLASS. KILL. BLUEBEARD'S FRIENDS.
    IMP.
HERE WE GO
HOTEL
ICECREAM
LIGHT SHINING IN BUCKINGHAMSHIRE
LOVE AND INFORMATION
MAD FOREST
A NUMBER
PIGS AND DOGS
SEVEN JEWISH CHILDREN
THE SKRIKER
THIS IS A CHAIR
THYESTES *after* Seneca
TRAPS
WHAT IF IF ONLY

Natasha Gordon
NINE NIGHT

Dave Harris
TAMBO & BONES

Jeremy O. Harris
'DADDY': A MELODRAMA
SLAVE PLAY

Sam Holcroft
COCKROACH
DANCING BEARS
EDGAR & ANNABEL
A MIRROR
PINK
RULES FOR LIVING
THE WARDROBE
WHILE YOU LIE

Branden Jacobs-Jenkins
APPROPRIATE
GLORIA
AN OCTOROON

Lucy Kirkwood
BEAUTY AND THE BEAST
    with Katie Mitchell
BLOODY WIMMIN
THE CHILDREN
CHIMERICA
HEDDA *after* Ibsen
IT FELT EMPTY WHEN THE HEART
    WENT AT FIRST BUT IT IS
    ALRIGHT NOW
LUCY KIRKWOOD PLAYS: ONE
MOSQUITOES
NSFW
RAPTURE
SMALL HOURS
TINDERBOX
THE WELKIN

Tony Kushner
ANGELS IN AMERICA –
    PARTS ONE AND TWO
CAROLINE, OR CHANGE
HOMEBODY/KABUL
THE VISIT, OR THE OLD LADY
    COMES TO CALL
    after Friedrich Dürrenmatt

Kimber Lee
UNTITLED F*CK M*SS S**GON PLAY

Bruce Norris
CLYBOURNE PARK
DOWNSTATE
THE LOW ROAD
THE PAIN AND THE ITCH
PURPLE HEART

Lynn Nottage
CLYDE'S
CRUMBS FROM THE TABLE OF JOY
INTIMATE APPAREL
MLIMA'S TALE
RUINED
SWEAT

Jack Thorne
2ND MAY 1997
AFTER LIFE *after* Hirokazu Kore-eda
BUNNY
BURYING YOUR BROTHER IN
    THE PAVEMENT
A CHRISTMAS CAROL *after* Dickens
THE END OF HISTORY...
HOPE
JACK THORNE PLAYS: ONE
JACK THORNE PLAYS: TWO
JUNKYARD
LET THE RIGHT ONE IN
    after John Ajvide Lindqvist
THE MOTIVE AND THE CUE
MYDIDAE
THE SOLID LIFE OF SUGAR WATER
STACY & FANNY AND FAGGOT
WHEN WINSTON WENT TO WAR WITH
    THE WIRELESS
WHEN YOU CURE ME
WOYZECK *after* Büchner

debbie tucker green
BORN BAD
DEBBIE TUCKER GREEN PLAYS: ONE
DIRTY BUTTERFLY
EAR FOR EYE
HANG
NUT
A PROFOUNDLY AFFECTIONATE,
    PASSIONATE DEVOTION TO
    SOMEONE (– *NOUN*)
RANDOM
STONING MARY
TRADE & GENERATIONS
TRUTH AND RECONCILIATION

Annie Baker

INFINITE LIFE

NICK HERN BOOKS
London
www.nickhernbooks.co.uk

A Nick Hern Book

Infinite Life first published in Great Britain as a paperback original in 2023 by Nick Hern Books Limited, The Glasshouse, 49a Goldhawk Road, London W12 8QP, by special arrangement with Theatre Communications Group, Inc., New York

Infinite Life copyright © 2023 Annie Baker

Annie Baker has asserted her right to be identified as the author of this work

Cover illustration by Sam Green; art direction and design by National Theatre Graphic Design Studio

Designed and typeset by Nick Hern Books, London
Printed in the UK by Mimeo Ltd, Huntingdon, Cambridgeshire PE29 6XX

A CIP catalogue record for this book is available from the British Library

ISBN 978 1 83904 277 5

CAUTION   All rights whatsoever in this play are strictly reserved. Requests to reproduce the text in whole or in part should be addressed to the publisher.

Performing Rights   Applications for performance, including readings and excerpts, by amateurs and professionals should be addressed to Rachel Viola, United Talent Agency, 888 Seventh Avenue, 9th Floor, New York, NY 10106, *email* ViolaR@unitedtalent.com, *tel.* +1-212-659-2600

No performance of any kind may be given unless a licence has been obtained. Applications should be made before rehearsals begin. Publication of this play does not necessarily indicate its availability for performance.

www.nickhernbooks.co.uk/environmental-policy

Infinite Life was originally a co-production between the National Theatre and Atlantic Theater Company, and first performed at the Linda Gross Theater, New York City, on 15 August 2023, before transferring to the Dorfman auditorium of the National Theatre, London, on 30 November 2023 (previews from 22 November). The cast was as follows:

EILEEN	Marylouise Burke
YVETTE	Mia Katigbak
SOFI	Christina Kirk
GINNIE	Kristine Nielsen
ELAINE	Brenda Pressley
NELSON	Pete Simpson
Director	James Macdonald
Set Designer	dots
Costume Designer	Ásta Bennie Hostetter
Lighting Designer	Isabella Byrd
Sound Designer	Bray Poor
Props Designer	Noah Mease
Movement Director	Sasha Milavic Davies
Wig Designer and Original Make-up Design	Alfreda 'Fre' Howard
Casting	David Caparelliotis CSA, Joseph Gery CSA
Associate Director, Atlantic Theater Company	Caitlin Ryan O'Connell
Associate Sound Designer	Nathan Rubio
Staff Director, National Theatre	Georgia Green

Marylouise Burke, Mia Katigbak, Christina Kirk, Kristine Nielsen, Brenda Pressley and Pete Simpson appeared with the permission of Equity UK, incorporating the Variety Artistes' Federation, pursuant to an exchange programme between American Equity and Equity UK.

Characters

SOFI, *forties, lives in Los Angeles, California*
EILEEN, *seventies, lives in Wichita, Kansas*
ELAINE, *sixties, lives in Dublin, New Hampshire*
GINNIE, *sixties, lives in Rio Vista, California*
YVETTE, *sixties/seventies, lives in Midland, Michigan*
NELSON, *forties, lives in San Francisco, California*

Setting

A clinic two hours north of San Francisco.

May 2019.

/ is an interruption and indicates when the next line of dialogue should begin.

This text went to press before the end of rehearsals and so may differ slightly from the play as performed.

1

A sunny day. A row of outdoor chaises longues. SOFI *is sitting in one of them, reading.* EILEEN *enters with her water bottle and finds another chair a safe distance away.*

EILEEN. Hello.

SOFI. Hi!

    EILEEN *settles into her chair.*

EILEEN. Eileen.

SOFI. Sofi.

    A pause while EILEEN *finishes settling into her chair.*

EILEEN. I know a lot of Sophies.

SOFI. Really?

EILEEN. My daughter has three different friends named Sophie.

SOFI. Well mine is with an F.

EILEEN. An F?

SOFI. Like S-O-F-I instead of P-H-I-E.

EILEEN. Ohhh.

    Pause. EILEEN *wraps a rolled-up blue towel around her neck.*

SOFI. How old is your daughter?

EILEEN. Forty-four.

SOFI. That's a good age.

EILEEN. You couldn't possibly be forty-four.

SOFI. I'm forty-seven.

EILEEN. No!

SOFI. Mmhm.

EILEEN. You look great.

SOFI. Thank you.
    (*Pause.*)
    So do you.

  SOFI *goes back to her book.*

EILEEN (*without looking over at her again*). Are you married?

SOFI.…I am.

  Pause.

  Are you married?

EILEEN. I am.
    Almost fifty years.

SOFI. Wow.

  Beat. SOFI *picks up her book again. She has to go back a page to remember what she was reading. She reads for about ten seconds.*

EILEEN. What are you reading?

SOFI. Daniel Deronda.

EILEEN. Say that again?

SOFI. Daniel. Deronda.

EILEEN. Is it good?

SOFI. It's great. It's very weird and great.

EILEEN. Weird huh.

  Short pause.

SOFI. Are you reading anything right now?

EILEEN. I have a couple of books with me but I can't get into anything.

SOFI. Yeah I know the feeling.
 This one –
 This one if I'm not reading it all the time it seems really boring but once I'm into it it's like the most entertaining thing in the world. I have to be in the right head space.

EILEEN. Are you in the right head space now?

SOFI. I think so.

Silence for a while.

EILEEN. Are you fasting?

SOFI. Yes.

EILEEN. When did you start?

SOFI. Today.
 Are you?

EILEEN. Yup.

SOFI. When did you start?

EILEEN. Three days ago.

SOFI. How do you feel?

EILEEN. *Great.*

SOFI. Great.

EILEEN. How do you feel?

SOFI. Hungry.

EILEEN. That goes away.

SOFI. Oh great.

EILEEN. It's hard to focus on one thing, like a book.

SOFI. Yeah. I was think/ing that it –

EILEEN. But my mind feels very clear.

Pause.

 Where are you from?

SOFI. Los Angeles.

EILEEN. Los Angeles!

SOFI. Have you been?

EILEEN. Yes. My daughter and I lived there when she was a teenager. My other daughter.

SOFI. Huh.

EILEEN. She was a very serious classical violinist as / a child –

SOFI. Oh wow.

EILEEN. And we moved out there so she could study with the best teacher in the country. Ron Glatzer. Have you heard of him?

SOFI *shakes her head no.*

I wanted her to study with him and also really see what that world was like because we didn't have any kind of exposure to anything like it in Wichita. Anyway she hated the whole scene and she decided not to become a violinist!

SOFI. Oh.

I guess good for her.

EILEEN. We lived fifteen minutes from downtown but on some mornings it would take an hour and a half and I remember thinking while we sat in the car: this is a nightmare. I'm living in a nightmare.

SOFI. Yeah the traffic can be hellish.

EILEEN. It's terrible!

SOFI. Yeah.

ELAINE enters, carrying a canvas bag.

EILEEN. Look who it is.

ELAINE. I slept for eleven hours.

EILEEN. That's good.

ELAINE. I hope so.

She finds a chair.

EILEEN. How are you feeling?

ELAINE. I feel exhausted but my mind is very alert.

EILEEN. That's what I was just saying. This is Sofi.

ELAINE. Hello Sofi. I'm Elaine.

SOFI. Hi Elaine.

> ELAINE *keeps her chair flat so she's facing the sky. She takes out a cloth and puts it over her face to shield it from the sun. They all stay that way for a while.* SOFI *finally goes back to her book. About thirty seconds later,* GINNIE *enters with her water bottle. For some reason nobody says hello to her and she doesn't say hello to anyone. She takes a while picking her chair. She settles in, she adjusts. She is still.*

Twenty minutes later.

2

Twenty minutes later. ELAINE *has lifted up the cloth over her face to talk to* GINNIE.

GINNIE. No there's more than one sphincter.

ELAINE. I thought it / was –

GINNIE. There's your anal sphincter but there's also your cardiac sphincter and your pyloric sphincter. That's why carbonation makes you feel good. It activates your pyloric sphincter.

ELAINE. Isn't it bad for your bones?

GINNIE. What? Carbonation?

ELAINE. I heard it's bad for your bones. I have osteoporosis and my daughter in law said to stop drinking seltzer.

GINNIE. I've never heard of that.
Does she mean soda? Junky soda?

ELAINE. No she said just plain carbonation is bad for your bones.

Pause. GINNIE *sips the seltzer, a little sad about this possibility.*

GINNIE. Well it helps with the nausea.

ELAINE. You're still nauseous?

GINNIE *nods.* ELAINE *puts the cloth back over her face. They are quiet for a while.*

GINNIE. We also have tiny sphincters in our eyes.

(*To* SOFI.) What are you here for?

SOFI *is engaged, or at least pretending to be engaged, in Daniel Deronda.*

ELAINE. Sofi she's talking to you.

SOFI. Oh.

SOFI *puts down her book.*

Sorry.

GINNIE. What are you here for? You're so young.

SOFI. I'm not so young. Um – I'm here for a pain thing.

GINNIE. What kind of pain thing?

SOFI. A chronic pain thing.

GINNIE. Fibromyalgia?

SOFI. No.

GINNIE. What is it?

ELAINE. Ginnie she doesn't want to tell you.

GINNIE. She doesn't?

SOFI. Um maybe at some point? Maybe not now.

ELAINE (*from under the cloth*). She doesn't know you.

GINNIE *thinks, then nods.*

SOFI. What are you here for?

ELAINE*'s phone dings.*

GINNIE. I have autoimmune thyroid stuff but mostly I'm here for my vertigo.

SOFI. Huh.

ELAINE. I just got a very cute picture of my grandchildren.

She shows it to GINNIE.

GINNIE. Oh they're twins.

ELAINE. Identical twins and competitive gymnasts.

SOFI *gets up and carefully starts to walk away.*

Sofi where are you going?

SOFI. I forgot my phone and also I might take a nap.

GINNIE. Were we bothering you?

SOFI. No no. I just um – I just need to make a phone call and also I'm a little tired. I'll be back soon.

GINNIE. You can tell us to shut up.

SOFI. No no I don't want you to shut up.

SOFI *disappears. After she's gone:*

EILEEN (*eyes still closed*). She's from Los Angeles.

SOFI *re-enters.*

SOFI. ...I forgot my book.

She goes back to her chair. She picks up her book. She starts walking out again.

ELAINE. What are you reading?

EILEEN (*eyes still closed*). Daniel Deronda.

SOFI. Yeah Daniel Deronda.

ELAINE. I'm surprised you can focus.

SOFI. Well it's my first day.

ELAINE. Ohhh.   GINNIE. That makes sense.

YVETTE *enters.*

ELAINE. Yvette!

GINNIE. Yvette how are you feeling.

> YVETTE *finds her way into a chair. She has a green juice, sunglasses, a donut cushion, and a tiny purple electrical fan.*

YVETTE. …Much much better.

ELAINE. This is Sofi.
Sofi this is my roommate Yvette.

YVETTE. Hello Sofi.

SOFI. Nice meeting you. Um. I'll be right back. (*Exiting*.)
Five hours later.

3

Five hours later. Early evening into the beginning of sunset.
YVETTE *has turned on the little purple fan.*

YVETTE. – and this is her job because apparently she has a very sexy voice!

ELAINE. There are some things I would not want described to me.

> SOFI *re-enters.*

GINNIE. Sofi's back!

SOFI. Hello everyone.

EILEEN. That was a long phone conversation.

SOFI. Oh, well / I –

EILEEN. I'm kidding I'm kidding.

SOFI. I took a nap and I um…

> *She settles back down in a chair.*

What a nice night.

GINNIE. Sofi Yvette was just telling us about her cousin /
who –

YVETTE. Second cousin.

GINNIE. Who narrates pornography for blind people.

SOFI. Oh wow.
Like in person?

ELAINE. No no – .   GINNIE. In *person*?

YVETTE. No she makes these recordings and if you're blind
you can listen to them online. And she says, you know, okay,
now he's throwing her down on the bed / and –

Laughter from GINNIE *and* ELAINE.

EILEEN (*eyes closed*). Enough enough.

ELAINE. Have you listened to it?

YVETTE. I have not listened to it.

GINNIE. We should listen to it.

ELAINE. Ginnie.

YVETTE. I would *possibly* be willing to listen to it.

A pause.

SOFI. How um...
How does...
How much detail does she...

Pause. They all look at her.

I just feel like it would be difficult to, uh, talk about what
they were doing at the same time as you talked about what
they look like while they're doing it.

YVETTE. I don't get it.

GINNIE. We don't understand what you're talking about Sofi
but later we'll all listen to it and you can find out.

They all gaze out at the sunset for a while.

ELAINE. I don't know if I want to listen to it.
I find that stuff very depressing.

GINNIE. I think it's a generational thing.

ELAINE. Pornography?

GINNIE. I think so.

They all look at SOFI *again.*

Sofi.

SOFI. Yes.

GINNIE. Do you think it's a generational thing?

EILEEN. Stop Ginnie.

GINNIE. What?

EILEEN (*eyes still closed*). We're all a little high because we've been fasting for days so please ignore us.

GINNIE. She doesn't have to answer if she doesn't want to!

SOFI. I'm not that much younger than –
(*She thinks.*)
Do I think it's a generational thing? Pornography? Yeah maybe.
I'd say half the women I know watch pornography.

ELAINE. Half!   YVETTE. Half is a lot.

GINNIE. So it's a generational thing.

SOFI. I guess.

Pause.

I mean there's a lot of horrible stuff out there but what bothered me the most is that for years I couldn't find a single guy I thought was cute. They all looked like these enormous idiot rapists.

Pause.

GINNIE. And / then –

THREE   17

SOFI. And then I finally found this guy – this actor I guess you could call him – I mean he's still pretty cheesy – but I finally found this guy I think is cute and now I just type his name into whatever and I just watch him you know just um fuck whomever he happens to be fucking.

EILEEN *slowly gets to her feet.*

Oh no.

EILEEN. It's fine I had to go to the powder room anyway.

EILEEN *leaves.*

GINNIE. She's very Christian. She's a...
I forget.

YVETTE. I didn't know that!

ELAINE (*taking out her coloring book*).
She doesn't like people to curse around her.

YVETTE. So why were we talking about pornography?

SOFI. I feel terrible.

GINNIE. Don't, you didn't know and it was my fault anyway.

Silence. They all look at the moon, except ELAINE *who is coloring.*

YVETTE. What are you here for, Sofi?

SOFI Oh –

GINNIE. She doesn't want to talk about it.

SOFI. No. It's fine.
Um.
There's something wrong with my bladder.

YVETTE. Oh I had bladder stuff. I had bladder stuff for years.

SOFI. Really?

YVETTE *nods.*

How did you – how did you treat it?

YVETTE. I had my bladder removed.

ELAINE. You didn't tell me that!

YVETTE. It was a godsend.

SOFI. I didn't know you could do that.

YVETTE. I know it sounds terrible but it was a godsend.

SOFI. Is that why you came here?

YVETTE. Oh no.

GINNIE. Yvette's got a whole story.

YVETTE. Everyone has already heard my story.

ELAINE. You can tell it again. I've got my coloring book.

SOFI. Eighteen minutes later.

4

Eighteen minutes later.

YVETTE. – because I think when they did the C-section they nicked my bladder or something. Suddenly I'm peeing every fifteen, every twenty minutes. I remember trying to drive to the grocery store with my children strapped in the backseat – this is a ten-minute drive – and having to pull over by the side of the road and pee in the bushes.
And then I wean my daughter and my hormones change again and all my lupus symptoms come back! So I have two little kids and joint pain and night sweats and a rash on my face the shape of a butterfly and a bladder the size of a pea and I'm starting to realize that my husband is useless to me. So they do this thing called – what was it called – did they do this to you? They fill your bladder up with lidocaine and they distend / it –

SOFI. Instillations.

YVETTE. Yeah. Did that work for you?

SOFI. No.

YVETTE. That worked for me. For a few months. But then I got the urinary tract infection from hell. I think I got it from the instillations because every time they did it they catheterized me! And I keep testing positive for infection over and over again and they put me on bactrim, they put me on cipro, they put me on two months of doxy, they put me on every antibiotic imaginable and it doesn't go away. What year of my life is this. I think I'm thirty-seven. And I go to my doctor and I say 'there is an option you're not telling me about. there's a last-ditch effort. I can't do this for the rest of my life.' and he says 'well, Yvette, the last-ditch effort is to literally remove your bladder.' And I say 'let's do it. Put me on the books for tomorrow. It is of no use to me anymore.' And he says, you're gonna be living with a pouch for the rest of your life. And I said, great. I mean that's how bad it was. I said, a pouch sounds fantastic.

She realizes it's dark.

When did it get so dark?
What time is it?

SOFI *looks at her phone.*

SOFI. It's eight thirty-five.

ELAINE. I think Ginnie is asleep.

YVETTE. Okay. Long story short. Long story very short. They take my bladder out and I get a bodywide fungal infection from all the antibiotics I've been on and the fungus gets into my lungs and it's resistant to all the normal antifungals, it's resistant to clotrimazole and econazole and fluconazole and ketoconazole and itraconazole and voriconazole and they have to give me a life-threatening last resort antifungal that's not a zole and I'm in the hospital hooked up to an IV drip for two weeks. And then things get better and I can finally go back to work but then one day I'm sitting at my desk, I'm looking at the computer, and this grey shade goes down over my left eye. I mean I watch it go down. Like the end of a movie or something. And what do you know I've gone blind in my left eye. No explanation.

And then at some point I realized my lunulae had disappeared. Do you know what those are?

SOFI *shakes her head no.*

The half moons at the bottom of your fingernails. My lunulae had disappeared.
And then my arthritis came back.
And the brain fog.
And the difficulty swallowing.
And the scleroderma.
And the lichenplanus.
And the spondylosis.
And the labyrinthitis.
And the polymyositis.
And the pericarditis.
Then I got an MRI when I turned fifty-five and I'll never forget the doctor walking in and saying well Yvette it turns out in addition to all your other problems you have three herniated discs, multiple spurs, and osteoporosis.
So I had to accept it. I had to accept being in pain all the time.
(*Pause.*)
And then two years later I got diagnosed with breast cancer. And this is when the miracle happens. They want me to do chemo but then I hear about this water fasting clinic in California! An affordable place with real doctors. A friend of mine with fibromyalgia came here for thirteen days and she did what Erkin said and the pain was gone by the time she left. And I start hearing about how people reverse type 2 diabetes and how tumors magically disappear and I decide before I start chemo I'm gonna take charge of my life and come here first. So I come here and I fast for three whole weeks and at the end of the three weeks the tumor is gone.

SOFI. Really?

YVETTE. I have the pictures to prove it. And all the doctors back in Michigan say 'it's a miracle,' and I say 'you can call it a miracle, but I just cleansed my entire system for the past three weeks.' And I also lost twenty pounds.

SOFI. Wow.

FOUR   21

YVETTE. So I am this place's number one fan. I mean, I've told them, you should put me on the website. I don't know why they haven't put me on the website.

ELAINE (*still coloring*). They should.

SOFI. So why are you here this time?

YVETTE. The cancer is back.
Yeah eight years later the cancer is back. And this time they're saying we have to do chemo and a double mastectomy but I told them, let me go back and see Erkin. And then you can do whatever you want to me. But Erkin said I have to do juice this time not water. So I'm doing juice. But he says juice can work. So that's the plan.
(*Pause.*)
And then I told you, or maybe this was Elaine's story, or maybe this was Ginnie's story, about how right before I came here I had a dream about a morgue in an old stone building, a place that hadn't been opened for centuries. There were tiny windows covered in dirt. I walked down the stone steps and went inside. I pulled out a shelf. There was a dead body. A dead girl. I told this dream to my massage therapist and she said see, that's progress. You walked in there. You've never been brave enough to go inside the morgue before.

Silence.

ELAINE. Well, I just finished my drawing. I think this one took me three whole days.

SOFI. Can I see?

ELAINE *holds it up.* SOFI *and* YVETTE *lean forward to see it.* GINNIE *is still asleep.*

And then we all went to bed.

Everyone leaves.

Six hours later.

5

The middle of the night. SOFI *wanders onstage. She's silently crying. She wanders among the chairs. She buckles down at one point and touches the seat of a chair, unable to stand. She looks at her phone, she keeps crying. Eventually she dials a number and waits.*

SOFI. Hi you're not responding to any of my texts so I'm –
(*She starts stiflingly sobbing again.*)
I guess my question for you is:
If the person you were in love with doesn't exist anymore where did she go?
(*Pause.*)
I mean if she wasn't me then who was she? I mean can you *please tell me who she was*?

She hangs up. She squats on the ground for a little while, wondering if she'll cry again. Then she sits on a chair. She dials the number again.

I don't wish you were in this pain but I wish you could feel it for five seconds and know that that's what it's like for me twenty-four hours a day. I think I might be going crazy.

She hangs up and looks up at the moon. She breathes. Time passes. She is a little bit calmer. She dials a different number and sounds like a different person, or the same person in a different year of her life.

Hey it's Sofi.
I had this dream last night – you were fitting the tip of a tortilla chip into my asshole and it felt incredible. It's not something it would have ever occurred to me to do but now I want you to do it to me. I hope the conference went well.

She hangs up and looks at the moon again.

Eight hours later.

6

Eight hours later. The next morning. SOFI *hasn't moved.* GINNIE *enters.*

GINNIE. Morning.

SOFI. Good morning.

GINNIE. Sleep well?

SOFI. Not really.

GINNIE. Sleep is important.

SOFI. My roommate is really nice / but –

GINNIE. Who's your roommate?

SOFI. Janet.

> GINNIE *doesn't know who Janet is.* SOFI *makes a gesture to indicate Janet's hair.*

GINNIE. Ah.

SOFI. She's very sweet but she never leaves and she snores a lot.

GINNIE. A private room is only fifty bucks more a night.

SOFI. ... Yeah.

> GINNIE *settles in and takes out her make-up case.*

> What type of tree is that?
> (*Pointing.*)
> Next to the fence.

GINNIE. It looks like some kind of manzanita.

They regard the manzanita for a while.

SOFI. I don't think we have those in LA.

Pause.

GINNIE. I remember the first time I came to Northern California. It was just for two nights on a job. But on the way to the hotel we drove through a eucalyptus grove. I mean I didn't know it was a eucalyptus grove. I just smelled it through the window

and I said that's the best thing I've ever smelled in my life.
And then I said: I'm going to live here one day.

SOFI. And do you?

GINNIE. Kind of. I live in Rio Vista.

SOFI. Do you live in a eucalyptus grove?

GINNIE. No but I live a ten-minute drive away from one.

SOFI. What do you do for – Sorry.

SOFI *bends her head down to try to get some blood into it*.

GINNIE. I'm a flight attendant. Soon to be retired.
Are you feeling light headed?

SOFI *nods*.

Today's your second day?

SOFI *nods again*.

My second day was my worst. No my third day was my worst. I was throwing up bile. Have you thrown up yet?

SOFI *shakes her head no*.

If you do that's a good thing. You're literally puking up toxins. There was this guy here last / week –

SOFI. There was a guy?

GINNIE. Sometimes there are guys. And he was a Vietnam vet and apparently during Vietnam the army doctor gave him these horrible antibiotics for something and when he came here last week and started throwing up he said he could *taste the antibiotics in his mouth*. That same taste.

SOFI. Jesus.

GINNIE. And he loved it. He said, I'm finally getting this shit out of my system.

Pause.

Anyway day two and three are the worst.

GINNIE *starts putting on her make-up while looking in her compact. First she puts on a light layer of foundation.*

Then eyeliner. Then mascara. She's very good at it. SOFI *watches her. It's kind of spellbinding. After a while:*

SOFI. I'm normally a really healthy person.

GINNIE. Excuse me?

SOFI. I mean I've always been a really healthy person.

Pause.

GINNIE. Okay.

Pause.

Why do you want me to know that?

Pause while GINNIE *begins to apply a very subtle nude lipstick.*

It's a real trip right? It's a real identity crisis.

EILEEN *enters.*

Hi Eileen.

EILEEN. Hello all.

She moves slowly to her seat.

GINNIE. How are you feeling?

EILEEN. I feel fantastic.

EILEEN *stops right before she gets to her seat and slowly bends over, hands on her knees. It's unclear why she's stopping.* GINNIE *comes over and helps ease her into her chair.*

GINNIE. Hey hey hey.

EILEEN *gets into a lying down position.*

Maybe you should stay in bed today.

EILEEN. I'm fine.

SOFI *(to* GINNIE*)*. Should I get Bashka?

GINNIE. Who's Bashka?

SOFI. The nurse on call.
 I think she said her name was Bashka.

GINNIE. Bashka? Really?

EILEEN. I don't need anything. I'm fine.

GINNIE (*to* SOFI). This is normal.

They all go back to their seats. EILEEN *lies there and breathes. They watch* EILEEN *for a little while.*

You know I didn't have the crisis when I got sick but I had it when I realized I was never going to have children. It really took me by surprise.
It was like shedding an entire skin and it was the most painful thing that had ever happened to me. And then once I had shed the skin – I mean it took three years – but once I had shed the skin I was fine.

Pause.

Do you have any? Children?

SOFI. No.
Twenty-two hours later.

7

Twenty-two hours later. The next morning.

GINNIE. It's colder today!
I might need a blanket!
Eileen and Sofi do either of you want a blanket?

They shake their heads no.

I can't decide whether or not to get a blanket.

YVETTE *enters*.

Good morning.

YVETTE. There was another.

GINNIE. Another what?

YVETTE. Another school shooting.

GINNIE. Oh no.

SOFI *gets up*.

Where are you going?

SOFI. I don't feel so good. I think I'm gonna go lie in bed.

GINNIE. That's a good idea. YVETTE. Good for you.
Day three is the worst.

As SOFI *starts to exit:*

GINNIE. Don't be afraid to puke! Puking is good!

ELAINE *enters*.

ELAINE. I don't think puking is good.

SOFI (*while exiting*). Eleven hours later.

8

Eleven hours later. It's evening. EILEEN *is in her chair.* GINNIE, YVETTE *and* ELAINE *stand or sit around her.* EILEEN *is quite calm.*

EILEEN. This is the night you heard me screaming.
  You walked out of your room and the three of them were already here with me.

  SOFI *re-enters and watches from a distance*.

  I said terrible things.
  I said: why does everyone hate me? I said why does Erkin hate me.
  They said Eileen try to tell us about the pain
  And I said well ladies the pain feels like hellfire.
  I said none of you have ever been in this much pain.
  They said how do you know Eileen

And I said I can tell by looking at you.
I said: why did Erkin only spend fifteen minutes talking to me and an hour talking to Elaine?
I said it's a conspiracy.
I said Ginnie you're doing it wrong.
I said Sofi go away.
I said You're all useless to me.
I said no one should ever try to recreate this.
This is agony in its purest form.
A minute of this is an infinity.
I said don't ever tell anyone you saw me like this. And you said:
Okay.

SOFI. Eight hours after that.

9

The faint sounds of Northern California at night. SOFI is alone. She lies in one of the chairs and looks up at the moon and the stars. Then she looks at a few things on her phone. Then she dials a number.

SOFI. Hi it's Sofi.
Right now I'm picturing I'm lying on my back... and you're fucking my mouth... and I'm completely relaxing my... um... my throat sphincter and then you pull out and you start fucking my pussy. And then you alternate fucking my throat and my pussy and I'm screaming and you're screaming and I can taste myself on your cock and...

She starts to run out of ideas.

I'm slightly distracted because I can't remember if people actually have throat sphincters. I'm going to touch myself now.

She hangs up. She masturbates for a while, under her robe. She can't come. Also it hurts now.

Fuck.
FUCK

She dials a different number, waits, then:

Please call me back. Just call me back to let me know you're still alive. Call me back to let me know I'm still alive. Everything is horrible here. It used to be some kind of roadside motel. We sit in these lawn chairs and we all spend hours staring at a parking lot behind a bakery. I can smell the bread baking at five a.m. I spent all of today throwing up bile. And I don't think it's working.
Pete who are the normal happy people? They're out there. They're buying bread.

Silence.

I'm a nightmare. I'm living in a nightmare. This is a nightmare. I'm living in a nightmare.
This is a nightmare.
If you don't forgive me I want to be torn apart by wild animals.

She hangs up.

Seven hours later.

10

Morning. Bright sun. SOFI *is reading, or trying to read Daniel Deronda. It's pretty hard to focus. She's wearing sunglasses.*
NELSON *enters, shirtless, barefoot, in pants.* SOFI *tries not to look surprised. He lies down in one of the chairs, in one of the rows in front of her.*
He sunbathes.
She tries to stay cool and just read Daniel Deronda. She reads the same sentence over and over again.
After a very long time, not moving and with his eyes closed the whole time:

NELSON. What are you reading?

SOFI. It's a book called Daniel Deronda.

NELSON. What's it about?

SOFI. Well I'm only on page one hundred and fifty-two but so far it's about this girl named Gwendolyn who's – all the guys are in love with her and she's trying to figure out who to marry.

A long silence.

NELSON. Who's Daniel Deronda?

SOFI. Yeah I think he's actually the main character – we met him at the very beginning of the book – but he hasn't reappeared yet so I don't know that much about him.

He nods and continues sunbathing. She sits there. She tries to go back to Daniel Deronda. She reads the same sentence over and over again. Then she thinks: why not talk about that?

I keep reading the same sentence over and over again. It's kind of hard to focus because I'm on day four.

NELSON. What's the sentence?

SOFI. 'He had never admitted to himself that Gwendolyn might refuse him, but – heaven, help us all! – we are often unable to act on our certainties; our objection to a contrary issue (were it possible) is so strong that it rises like a spectral illusion between us and our certainty: we are rationally sure that the blind-worm cannot bite us mortally, but it would be so intolerable to be bitten, and the creature has a biting look – we decline to handle it.'

Pause.

Now that I've read it out loud it makes a little more sense.

He continues sunbathing. She waits for his response, then decides to keep reading. But now she is reading the next sentence over again. Finally she gives up. She puts the book in her lap, lies back, closes her eyes, and tries sunbathing. After a while he gets up and walks away. As he walks away, she turns her head to watch him go.

Twenty-five hours later.

11

ELAINE *and* YVETTE *and* GINNIE *are back, in mid-conversation.* SOFI *is half-listening.*

ELAINE. Almond flour and coconut flour and a cup of coconut or almond or hemp milk and a teaspoonful of manuka honey.

YVETTE. Manuka.

ELAINE. And a lot of eggs and baking powder.
I just make one at time and I make it with yogurt and blueberries instead of maple syrup.

GINNIE. Blueberries are my favorite berry. / Of all the berries.

ELAINE. You have to be so careful with blueberries though. I mean I eat a lot of them because we have a bush in our backyard but I only eat them in season.

YVETTE. There's this one grocery store near me that has great blueberries year round.

ELAINE. Organic?

YVETTE. I think so.

ELAINE. They couldn't be.

YVETTE. I think they're organic.

ELAINE. Not if it's year round. Blueberries are bad. Blueberries are some / of the biggest culprits.

YVETTE. I always wash them.

| ELAINE. That doesn't get it all off. | GINNIE. Sometimes I wash fruit in white vinegar. |

ELAINE. You also have to keep an eye out for labels that say 'organically grown.' Organically grown doesn't mean organic.

YVETTE. I read an article recently about how the amounts of pesticides are actually so small that it doesn't / really –

ELAINE. They're lying to you. It's a conspiracy. / It's a nationwide conspiracy.

32   INFINITE LIFE

YVETTE. It was by a scientist and it said the pesticide levels on non-organic produce were negligible. That was the word they used. And that if you just give it a / quick rinse –

ELAINE. But we're not just talking about the health of the people eating it. We're talking about the health of the soil, the health of the farm workers in Mexico, we're talking about the people who pick these blue/berries every day –

YVETTE. Do they grow blueberries in Mexico?

GINNIE. I remember the one time I went to Mexico we kept driving past all these fields and I kept asking 'what are they growing' and finally someone told me: canteloupes. Apparently all the canteloupes in the world are from Mexico.

Pause.

Oh no wait I've never been to Mexico. I'm talking about Costa Rica.

ELAINE *is trying to collect herself.*

ELAINE. Once every year for twenty years I've been visiting this middle school to give my puberty talk and five years ago they started asking me if I could also go to the elementary school and start talking to the third- and fourth-graders because a lot of the eight-year-olds have already gotten their period. Eight-year-olds.
(*Short pause.*)
That's pesticides.
That's endocrine disruption.
That's people saying oh it's no big deal it's negligible amounts but it's negligible amounts over an entire childhood, an entire lifetime, and look at us we're all sick.

Pause.

GINNIE. You know what I think is making everyone sick?
   (*She waits, then.*)
   Bad sex.

ELAINE. I don't want to joke around, Ginnie.

GINNIE. But I'm not joking.

YVETTE. How did we start talking about this?

GINNIE. You asked her about her gluten-free pancake recipe.

ELAINE *takes out her coloring book.*

SOFI. Did any of you notice a guy here yesterday?

Pause.

YVETTE. A man?

SOFI. Yeah this shirtless man walking around.

They all shake their heads no.

I think maybe I hallucinated him. Like a fasting-induced hallucination.

GINNIE. Was he cute?

SOFI. Yeah he was kind of weirdly cute.

While drawing, eyes on the page:

ELAINE. Tell us about your husband Sofi.

Short pause.

SOFI. What do you want to know? I mean he's great.

YVETTE. What's his name.

SOFI. Peter. Pete.

ELAINE. What does he do for work?

SOFI. He's a –

SOFI *shifts in her chair to get more comfortable. They're all watching her.*

Pete is wonderful but we're actually separated right now. It's hopefully temporary.

YVETTE. Separated.

SOFI. Yeah.

YVETTE. I'm so sorry.

SOFI. Yeah.

YVETTE. Was he not understanding about your illness?

SOFI. No he's been very understanding.
   (*Short pause.*)
   It's my fault.
   I'm just like a really shitty person and instead of making me a better person being sick has made me even shittier.

ELAINE. No Sofi. YVETTE. That can't be true.

GINNIE. Why do you think you're a shitty person?

NELSON appears, still shirtless but this time in baggy silky pants. They all look up. He's a little surprised to see all four of them looking at him.

NELSON. Hey.

GINNIE. Hi. ELAINE. Hello. YVETTE. Welcome.

He finds the farthest chair away from them and stretches out his body like a cat. They all sit in silence, playing it cool.
ELAINE draws in her coloring book.

GINNIE. What were we just talking about.

No one answers. She remembers.

Ah.

His stretched-out-cat body seems to be radiating light and they're all trying not to look at it, except for GINNIE, *who is less afraid of looking.*
YVETTE takes out a book and starts reading it.

What are you reading, Yvette?

YVETTE shows her the cover.

YVETTE. Have you heard of it?

GINNIE shakes her head no.

Oh it's great. It's great. Elaine you should check it out because the woman who wrote it has chronic Lyme too. And endometriosis and Sjögren's and uh… something else too I forget the name of it. That's not what it's really about though.

She flips through the book to try to find it but then gives up.

It's a memoir. The author's parents were Holocaust survivors so there was a lot of family trauma and then when she grew up she joined this cult that she didn't realize was a cult until decades later when she'd already given them all her life savings so at forty-five she left the cult and changed her name and started working at Applebee's. And the whole time she was dreaming about this white water rafting business she wanted to start with her best friend from childhood. So she saved up all her waitressing money and that's when she realized she had chronic Lyme and after she kicked the Lyme she and her friend finally *did* start this white water rafting company in Colorado and it was a huge hit because it was run entirely by women well not *because* but being run by women was part of its mission. And now she's married to the love of her life and there's also all this great stuff in it about stepparenting that you
(*To* GINNIE.)
might find interesting.
I think she's very smart about it.

SOFI. You have stepkids?

GINNIE *nods*.

GINNIE. My girlfriend has a son.

YVETTE. It's also sort of a how-to guide about starting your own business.

NELSON *changes position. After a long time:*

NELSON. I think my aunt went to high school with that lady.

They are all speechless.

That all sounds really familiar and I remember my aunt saying she wrote a book about it.

YVETTE. Huh.   GINNIE. Wow.

Pause.

GINNIE. What's your name?

NELSON. Me? Nelson.

YVETTE. Nelson.

Pause.

GINNIE. I'm Ginnie and this is Yvette and Sofi and Elaine.

NELSON (*eyes still closed*). Hey.

GINNIE. Where are you coming from?

NELSON. Noe Valley.

GINNIE. Oh you're a local like me.

NELSON. I wouldn't really call this local.

GINNIE. I mean compared to these gals.

Silence.

What do you do for work?

Silence.

NELSON. Ah you know what? I don't mean to be a dick but I promised myself I wouldn't talk about work while I was here.

GINNIE. Sure. Sure.

GINNIE *gives the other women a significant look. Then she takes out her compact and applies a layer of lipstick.* SOFI *and* YVETTE *pretend to read;* ELAINE *colors.*
After a minute or two, NELSON*'s phone rings. He answers, with Facetime.*

NELSON. Hey.

A WOMAN'S VOICE. Hi!

NELSON. Hold on let me go somewhere private.

He leaves. They all sit, absorbing what just happened.

SOFI. Where's Eileen?

YVETTE. She's having a hard time.

SOFI. Thirteen hours later.

12

Midnight. SOFI *is standing in the dark in the middle of the night, looking at her phone.* NELSON *walks onstage and starts vaping, far away from her.*

SOFI. Are you water fasting or just doing juice?

NELSON. Fasting.

SOFI. Doesn't the nicotine make you sick?

NELSON. It's weed.

SOFI. Oh.

NELSON. It's for pain. I'll stop tomorrow.

He vapes, she looks at her phone.

What day are you?

SOFI. Five.

NELSON. How do you feel?

SOFI. Terrible.
People keep saying they feel great but I feel like I have the flu and I'm still thinking about food all the time.

NELSON. Yeah.

SOFI. I keep thinking about turkey meatballs.

Pause.

You're day two?

NELSON. Yeah.

SOFI. How is it?

NELSON. It's all right. I've done it before. But just for a weekend.

SOFI. How many days are you gonna do it for this time?

NELSON. Twenty-four.

SOFI. Whoa.
Is that safe?

NELSON. I know a guy who did thirty-six.

SOFI. Did it help him?

NELSON. Oh yeah.

Silence.

How's Daniel Defoe?

Pause.

SOFI. It's good. I can't really read it anymore though. My mind is...
(*A gesture.*)

NELSON. Yeah.

SOFI. Gwendolyn made a really bad decision like right before I had to stop reading and now I have to wait to find out the um consequences of her decision.

NELSON. How many days are you doing?

SOFI. Erkin says I should do at least eight to ten. I don't know if I'm gonna make it.

NELSON (*mildly*). You can do it.

He vapes.

SOFI. What kind of pain are you in?

Silence.

NELSON. My fucking colon.

SOFI. Huh.

NELSON. Yeah it's not like the sexy kind of pain.

The thought of his colon is wildly sexy.

SOFI. ...I don't know.

NELSON. What do you have? Some kind of autoimmune thing?

SOFI. Why do you say that?

NELSON. I just feel like everyone here has some kind of autoimmune thing that makes them tired all the time.

SOFI. No.
>I have a pain thing.
>I mean maybe it's autoimmune.
>But I'm not tired. I'm like the opposite of tired. I've been sleeping like two hours a night.

NELSON. What's your pain thing?

She makes a split-second decision to tell him everything.

SOFI. Whenever I pee it's like I'm peeing razors. And my bladder is covered in these ulcers and there's always blood in my urine. And for the past five months my um clitoris has been in constant pain and it's like someone is diddling me too hard but not making me cum like twenty-four hours a day. Apparently it's not that uncommon but no one talks about it and doctors don't understand it or what causes it.

Pause.

NELSON. Shit man.

SOFI. And when I do cum the pain afterwards is excruciating.

Pause.

>It seems like a joke, right?

NELSON. What?

SOFI. Like some punishment or something. In a fairy tale. The witch cursed me.

Pause.

NELSON. The witch, huh.

SOFI. Yeah the witch.

She begins to regret telling him what she just told him.
Pause, after some vaping:

NELSON. There was this one night. I got a blockage cuz of all this scar tissue that had built up. But I didn't know that at the time. Basically I needed to shit but I couldn't so I was lying on the bathroom floor and I don't want to sound like a dick but I highly doubt you have ever experienced the level of pain that I'm talking about. I couldn't move and then I started puking because that was the only way it could leave my body so it just started coming out of my throat and I was shitting through my mouth into the toilet. And I was like: so this is what my shit tastes like. And then I was like: you can't tell me this isn't a metaphor.

SOFI. And what was the metaphor?

NELSON. I don't know, man. The metaphor is that shit was coming out of my mouth.

Long pause.

I don't know if you've been through childbirth but I met this lady who had the same thing happen to her and she said it was way worse than childbirth.

Pause.

SOFI. I have not been through childbirth.

Pause.

But like... you don't actually know if your level of pain that night was worse than my level of pain on my worst night. It's like impossible to know. / So I don't –

NELSON. No I know that's why I said I / doubted it but I didn't –

SOFI. So it's like I don't know what's the point of people saying that.
Like even childbirth I think is wildly different in how painful it is from person to person.

NELSON. Yeah yeah okay I know.

Pause.

SOFI. Have you ever been at a childbirth? At the birth of a child?

NELSON. Yeah I was with my wife when she gave birth to our daughter.

Pause.

SOFI. Cool.

Pause.

What's your wife…

Pause.

Sorry.
What's your wife's name?

NELSON. Ceridwen.

SOFI. Ceridwen.

NELSON. Yep.

SOFI. Nelson and Ceridwen.

NELSON. Yeah.

> SOFI *squats on the ground and breathes.*
>
> So like… do you not cum anymore?
>
> *She buries her face in her hands.*

SOFI. This is such a crazy conversation.

NELSON. I think it's cuz the moon is in Scorpio right now. And we're sitting under the moon.

SOFI. Um.
No. I cum.
I just have to pick and choose.
Like I have to make sure it's really worth the pain afterwards.

NELSON. Right.

SOFI. I used to cum all the time. That was like my specialty.

Pause.

It works the best if someone fucks me in the ass.

NELSON. Huh.

SOFI. Like it's the least painful. Or it's painful in a different way that I like.

NELSON. Does your uh… do you have a partner?

SOFI. I have a husband.

NELSON. Oh yeah?

SOFI. Yeah you didn't notice?

She holds up her hand.

NELSON. I can't see.

SOFI. I mean before. During the day.

NELSON. I guess I don't look for that kind of thing.

SOFI. I guess not.

Pause.

NELSON. Is your husband like understanding about all this stuff?

SOFI. He's been very understanding but also not that into talking about sex or trying different kinds of sex so a few months ago I started having this um I guess you could call it emotional although it's not particularly emotional affair with this guy I work with and we've never touched each other but we leave each other all these voicemails and texts about what we want to do to each other and it's the only thing that has honestly gotten me through the past year of being in pain and realizing we're never going to have a baby I mean I really feel like this guy saved my life, but then Pete – my husband – listened to one of his voice messages by accident – I mean that's what he said – but he heard one of the messages and it didn't seem to make a difference to him that this guy has never actually touched me or maybe he doesn't believe me when I tell him the guy has never actually touched me but anyway now we're spending some time apart. Temporarily. I hope.

NELSON. Oh man.

SOFI. And so my husband isn't speaking to me but I didn't even get to have sex with this other person. I just got six voicemails about it and I listen to them every night.

Pause.

NELSON. This is why Ceridwen and I have always had an open relationship.

A long pause.

SOFI. I think maybe all I'm looking for is a conversation like this. Just like...

(*A gesture of expanse and freedom.*)

NELSON. I should go back to bed.

SOFI. What's your prognosis?

NELSON. I've been clear for two years but I just went in three weeks ago and it's back. They want to do radiation again.

She nods.

It feels really good not to eat though. Like to know I'm not ingesting inflammatory crap. I keep picturing my colon like – I keep picturing this fresh new pink colon growing back. That's what I'm trying to meditate on.

SOFI. Healthy colons are pink?

NELSON. Oh yeah healthy colons are shiny and pink and smooth.

SOFI. And you know what your colon looks like?

NELSON. Yeah. I have all these pictures on my phone.

Pause.

SOFI. Can I see?

NELSON. You wanna see my colonoscopy photos?

SOFI. Yeah.

NELSON.... Okay.

He takes his phone out of his silky pants. He scrolls. It takes him a while. He pauses for a second.

This is my daughter.

SOFI (*smiling, in pain*). Cute.

NELSON. And...

Scrolling more.

Okay this is right before my diagnosis. That's my rectosigmoid junction.
And there it is.

SOFI. Oh wow.

NELSON. Four inches. Then...

He scrolls again.

This is six months after the surgery. They had to go through my stoma.

He shows her, then scrolls again.

And this is three weeks ago. See?

He points to something.

SOFI. Oh. Yeah.

Pause.

NELSON. It's called Primary Signet-Ring Cell Carcinoma with Peritoneal Dissemination.

She looks at him.

SOFI. Thank you for showing me.

NELSON. Sure.

SOFI. Are you in pain right now?

NELSON. Some. But the weed helped. Are you in pain right now?

SOFI. Yes.
The day after that.

13

SOFI *sits in her chair in the sun, dozing.* GINNIE *lies near her, also dozing, a green juice at her side.* EILEEN *enters. Now she's using a three-pronged cane to walk. She walks slowly.* SOFI *doesn't wake or pretends not to.*

EILEEN. You should be wearing sunglasses. Or a hat.

Pause.

You want a hat? Sofi.

SOFI (*eyes still closed*). Mm.

EILEEN. You want something to cover your eyes or your face? Like a hat?

SOFI. Sure.

EILEEN *turns around, slowly.*

(*Faintly.*) Oh you don't have to do that.

EILEEN *leaves.* SOFI *lies there. A minute passes.* EILEEN *eventually comes back with her cane and a cloth hat. She carefully places the hat on* SOFI*'s head, then sits down.*

The day after that.

14

The day after that. Everyone except NELSON. ELAINE *is holding a green juice and* GINNIE *is reading a Thich Nhat Hanh book.*

GINNIE. Here's a provocative question.

YVETTE. Ready.

GINNIE. I just finished a section of this book where the author tells a whole story about an Asian pirate / who –

ELAINE. An Asian pirate?

GINNIE. Yes an Asian pirate who rapes a fourteen-year-old girl.

ELAINE. I don't know if   YVETTE. Okay.
   I want to hear about this

GINNIE. He rapes her and she throws herself off the boat / and –

YVETTE. Off the pirate ship?

GINNIE. What?

YVETTE. Are they on a pirate ship?

GINNIE. No he's... *he's* a pirate and he takes over some other boat and he rapes this girl... anyway this is beside the point. There's this horrible guy and he rapes this little girl and then she kills herself.

YVETTE. Got it.

GINNIE. And Thich Nhat Hanh says:
   We are all the pirate and we are all the little girl.

Everyone absorbs this.

   We are all just as much capable of terrible things as we are goodness depending on our circumstances.

YVETTE. So what's the provocative question?

GINNIE. The question is...
   Do you believe that if you were raised under the same circumstances as this pirate, I mean born into the same family and the same poverty et cetera et cetera, that you would do the same thing?

ELAINE. So you're asking about nature versus nurture.

GINNIE. Well. Sort of.
   But he's also talking about compassion.

A pause.

YVETTE. Here's where I get stuck.

Pause.

   If I'm born in the same country as the pirate and into the same family and eat the same food and suffer the same abuse whatever / whatever...

GINNIE. Yeah...

YVETTE. Then I am the pirate.

Pause.

Aren't I just the pirate?

GINNIE. Yes. That's the point. If you were the pirate, would you do the same thing?

YVETTE. But I wouldn't be me. I'd be the pirate.

GINNIE. Right.

YVETTE. So I'd rape the girl because I'm me, the pirate.

GINNIE. But maybe you wouldn't.

YVETTE. But he did.
So I'm him.
So I rape the little girl.

GINNIE. Well that's a provocative answer.

ELAINE. I don't think I'd rape anyone under any circumstance.

YVETTE. Yes you would. Because you're the pirate.

GINNIE. Thus the dilemma.

YVETTE. No it's not a dilemma. It's a philosophical problem. Are you saying in this scenario it's the pirate but he's got the soul of Elaine?

GINNIE *thinks about this.*

Because then we're just talking about the existence of a soul. And that's a different question entirely.

Pause.

GINNIE. This is over my head.

YVETTE. Forget about it.

ELAINE *has been staring at her juice.*

GINNIE. First one?

ELAINE *nods.*

GINNIE. Sip it don't gulp it.
In thirty minutes you'll feel tremendous.

ELAINE. I don't want to feed the Lyme.

She keeps staring at her juice.

How long did Saint Francis fast for?

GINNIE. Forty days? YVETTE. Did Saint Francis fast?

ELAINE. Forty days is Jesus.

GINNIE. Oh right.

EILEEN, *who was seemingly asleep until now, speaks up without moving:*

EILEEN. Saint Francis fasted for forty days too.

Pause. ELAINE *takes a tiny sip.*

GINNIE. How does it feel?

ELAINE. Good.
It feels good.

15

A sunset. ELAINE *is almost done with her juice.*

GINNIE. Oh no it was the right thing in the end. He was a screamer, you know? Like a real scream in your face screamer.

YVETTE. I dated a screamer.

ELAINE. You know Craig used to be a screamer but then fifteen years ago we went to this retreat on a farm near Lake George run by this great couple and the man in the couple used to be a screamer and then he went into therapy and made these enormous changes so now they run these couples dialogue workshops on a tiny farm where you all share a bathroom and

I was on the verge of leaving Craig before we went and then
the retreat changed everything for us. We communicate in
a totally different way now.

SOFI. How is it different?

ELAINE. Well he signed this piece of paper that says if I say
this specific word sort of like a safe word it means he's
screaming at me. And he HAS to believe me and he HAS to
stop screaming. And I signed this other piece of paper saying
that I'll never say the word unless he's really truly screaming
and I'm really truly scared.

SOFI. What's the word?   YVETTE. And that worked?

ELAINE. It didn't work at first. He thought I was making it up.
That was part of the problem. He thought I was saying I was
scared to manipulate him so we had to go back to the farm
two more times and finally he got it into his head that I wasn't
locking myself in the bathroom to spite him, I was locking
myself in the bathroom because I was truly scared. And then
he started listening to me when I said it.
(*To* SOFI.)
The word was chimichanga.

YVETTE. Like / the –

ELAINE. But in the early days it was so silly. I'd say
chimichanga and he'd start screaming YOU CAN'T SAY
CHIMICHANGA or you know THAT DOESN'T MERIT
A CHIMICHANGA and it would actually make him even
more angry and scary.
(*She drinks more of the juice.*)
You know
(*To* GINNIE.)
you were right.
I feel tremendous.

It switches to late dusk, almost night. They are barely visible.

16

GINNIE. It's microwaves. It's *some* kind of wave. It's some kind of energy or wave from the moment the universe was created and that's the static you see on your television set. It's the Big Bang. It's actually energy from the Big Bang.

ELAINE. I think someone told you that and you believed them and now you're telling it to us.

GINNIE. No it was… I did a report on it in high school. Listen, listen. No energy can be destroyed. Energy just continues. It turns into sound energy, or light energy, and… the energy from the Big Bang has been radiating throughout the universe for millions of years. And then it uh… it turned into microwaves or some kind of wave and that thing, that static on the old televisions, that fuzz, that's the remnant of the Big Bang making itself known through your screen.
Because the energy has to go somewhere. It's ancient ancient energy.
Isn't that incredible? Remember it was Channel 3? Channel 3 was always the static. And that static was the Big Bang.

Everyone is dubious.

How crazy would I be to just be making this up.

It switches to night.

17

SOFI *picks up her cell phone and dials.*

SOFI. This is my last message.
 I hear that you need space.
 I hear that you need space.
 (*Pause.*)
 I thought I'd try to tell you what it's like.
 Instead of just saying I'm in pain I'm in pain feel bad for me Pete I'm in pain
 (*Pause.*)

It's like the center of a blow torch. It's also like throbbing.
It's like endless throbbing like throb throb throb throb like
tick tock tock endless into infinity time
That's wrong.
It's not like anything.
(*Pause.*)
You must think I'm a monster.
(*Pause.*)
Maybe I am a monster
My body is monstrous
My mind is monstrous
So I'm a monster.
Congratulations.
You married a monster.

She hangs up.

18

The next day. YVETTE *and* GINNIE *have gathered around* ELAINE, *who stands there in her traveling clothes with a suitcase on wheels.* SOFI *and* EILEEN *are still lying in their chaises longues.*

ELAINE. Well.

Pause.

YVETTE. What's the first thing you're going to do when you get home?

ELAINE. The first thing I have to do before I even get home is pick *this* one up from thyroid camp.

She gets out her phone, finds a photo of her cat, and shows it to them.

That's Tony.

SOFI. What's thyroid camp?

ELAINE. Last year he started developing all these thyroid problems that I thought were a hysterical response to my thyroid problems then it turns out it's a really big deal and he has to have this radioactive treatment and when he has it he has to be quarantined and can't be around people. So the week before I came here we dropped him off at this farm and on the way home I'm picking him up. He's been there for three whole weeks.

YVETTE. Does he get to play with the other radioactive cats?

ELAINE. Well that's what I was hoping but it turns out every cat is at a different stage of the three-week treatment at all times and they have to be kept apart so they don't contaminate each other.

GINNIE. Oh no.

ELAINE. Luckily they have something called a Kitty Kam and they give you this code and you can go to their website and type in your Kitty Kam code and watch your cat sleeping in his little cage. We thought it was so funny when they told us about it but I've been checking in on him every night before I go to sleep and Craig says he looks at it five or six times a day.

ELAINE puts the phone away.

...What happened to that man?

GINNIE. I heard he hasn't left his room.

They all look at SOFI.

SOFI. I haven't seen him.

Pause.

ELAINE. I wish you all luck on your... healing journeys. I wish that you all end up where you want to be on your healing journeys.

SOFI. Thank you Elaine.   GINNIE. Safe travels

ELAINE walks off. Her suitcase makes a rolling sound on what sounds like a gravel pathway offstage. The rolling sound gets fainter and fainter and fainter until it's gone.

They all stand there looking in the direction she walked off in.
They stand there for a while.

SOFI. Two days later
Maybe three days later? The end is a blur
I wasn't really thinking or seeing
I don't remember if I was there for nine days or ten or eleven
Ginnie left
Yvette left
My roommate Janet was still there
But mysteriously she had stopped snoring
She lay in bed silently all day and night. A couple of times I thought she had died.
New people stopped showing up because there was another wildfire approaching the town two towns away and everyone was getting scared.
I remember Janet wearing a scarf around her mouth and when I asked about it she said it was to prevent smoke inhalation but I couldn't smell any smoke anywhere. I could just smell the bakery across the parking lot.

19

SOFI *stands onstage with a suitcase. Or maybe she just has a huge backpack and a small duffel bag. The same bags she used to backpack around Europe in her twenties.*
EILEEN *is the only other person left onstage. She is in her chair, sleeping.*

SOFI. Eileen.

EILEEN *opens her eyes.*

I just wanted to say goodbye.

EILEEN. Oh Sofi! I had no idea you were leaving.

SOFI. Yeah sorry I didn't warn you.
(*Short pause.*)
Not that you needed to be warned.

EILEEN. Well. It's wonderful. That you're going home.

SOFI. When do you leave?

EILEEN. You know I'm not sure yet.
The pain is still quite bad and Erkin thinks it might be a good idea for me to keep going.
(*Pause.*)
This is my fourteenth day.

SOFI. I see.

EILEEN. How are you feeling?

SOFI. Mostly the same.

EILEEN. Ah.

NELSON *strolls out and squints in the sun. They are both surprised to see him. He is wearing a shirt for the first time. He stands there, facing out, hands on hips, squinting. They look at him, waiting for him to notice* SOFI *is wearing a backpack/carrying a bag. Eventually he notices.*

NELSON. Oh hey.

SOFI *nods.* EILEEN *slowly gets to her feet.*

SOFI. No, Eileen.

EILEEN. I just need to use the powder room.

EILEEN *walks out.* SOFI *stands there.* NELSON *stands there. But this time they're looking at each other.*

NELSON. It's weird you're leaving.

SOFI. Why?

He shrugs and just looks at her. Pause.

NELSON. Yeah. I'm just like… emerging. From day two to six.

SOFI. It can get pretty bad, right?

He shrugs.

How do you feel now?

NELSON. Great.

SOFI. Great.

Silence. They're still looking at each other.

NELSON. So where do you live?

SOFI. Los Angeles.

NELSON. Where / in –

SOFI. Cypress Park.

NELSON*'s never heard of it.*

NELSON. Do you have a job?

SOFI. Yes. I have a job.

Pause.

I'm the head of the Protein Strategy team at a meal kit delivery service.
(*Short pause.*)
I get a lot of free frozen meat.

NELSON. That's cool.

SOFI. And the hours are really good and the benefits are really good. And I get sixteen days of paid vacation. Which I'm using up right now. You have to tell me what you do now.

NELSON. I'm in Fintech.

SOFI. What's that?

NELSON. Financial. Technology.

SOFI. Oh Fin for Financial.

This whole thing is becoming unbearable. After a pause:

I uh... God.
I'm forty-seven and I still don't know how to do this.

They look at each other for a long time.

NELSON. Are you taking a plane back?

SOFI. Yes.

NELSON. When is your flight?

SOFI. It's at four.
But I need to leave at least two hours to get there.

NELSON. Why don't I call my wife and give her a heads-up and we can go to my room for a little while and see what happens.

A frozen silence. Then:

SOFI. You have to give her a heads-up?

NELSON. Yeah that's what we do.

Another silence.

SOFI. Well I like to leave a lot of time to get to the airport and I like to be there at least an hour forty minutes early.
I mean.
I can't. I want to so badly. You don't even know. But I can't.

NELSON. Cool.
(After a while.)
You know you probably don't want to *that* badly.
When people really want to do things they usually do them.

SOFI. Not me.

Pause.

I think the amount I want to is so far beyond your comprehension that you can't even... I think you can't even imagine the universe of what it feels like or looks like.

NELSON. I mean... okay.

SOFI. Also I would need like seven hours.
I would need to just have your cock in my mouth for like seven hours.

Pause.

NELSON. Seven hours sounds like too long, man. I'm gonna go take a nap.
If you change your mind come knock on my door and we can make out for ten minutes.

He starts walking out. Right before he's gone:

SOFI. Could I have one of those photos?

He doesn't understand at first.

NELSON. The –

Then he does.

Oh. Really?

She nods.

Why?
Or... uh... sure. Whatever.

He takes his phone out of his silky pants, then hesitates.

Look I start radiation again in three weeks so I can't really handle like intense / emotional contact with people who –

SOFI. I promise I won't text you and try to be your girlfriend. In fact I won't text you at all.

He scrolls through his pictures for a while, then finds them. Considering:

NELSON. More cancer or less cancer?

Pause.

SOFI. More?

NELSON. Here type in your number.

She types in her number, then hands the phone back to him. He sends the photo, puts his phone back in his pants.

SOFI. ...Good luck with everything.

NELSON. Yeah you too.

He walks out. She stands there for a while. Then she puts a hand on the left side of her chest under her breast. It's unclear, perhaps even to herself, if she's fondling herself or feeling her heartbeat or both. Then she sits on a chair. Maybe she's still wearing her enormous backpack. Then she looks at her phone. Not quite time to call the Uber. And then right after she calls the Uber she's going to have to pee at the last possible second before the long cab ride and then...

She looks at the photo NELSON *sent. After a while* EILEEN *walks back in. Then lies down very slowly. They are there,* EILEEN *lying down and* SOFI *sitting and wearing her backpack. After a little while:*

EILEEN. Are you all right, sweetheart?

SOFI *shrugs. After a pause:*

SOFI. Is what you have treatable?

EILEEN. It's called Complex Regional Pain Syndrome. It's in my nerves. There's not a cure but apparently sometimes it goes away. Sometimes it doesn't. It's not life-threatening.

SOFI. Yeah. Mine is kind of similar.

EILEEN. So I could be in this pain for the rest of my life or maybe a year from now things will be different.

SOFI. Yeah.

A long pause.

You know sometimes I actually do feel like it might be my fault.

EILEEN. Why do you think it's your fault?

SOFI. For not...
For not having lived the way I ought to have lived.
Not living the way I ought to be living.

EILEEN *nods*.

Do you think it's your fault?

EILEEN. Well for me it's a little complicated.
(*Short pause*.)
Maybe one of the others told you but for most of my life I've been a Christian Scientist.

SOFI. Oh! Wow. No. I didn't know.

EILEEN. I'm not sure what my relationship to it is right now – and I don't want you to make fun of it or say anything bad about it, / please –

SOFI. No no I wouldn't.

EILEEN. – but what I used to believe was not so much that one is being punished but that the pain and illness are just a signal that one has to get rid of an old way of thinking.

SOFI. In other words that it's your fault.

EILEEN. In other words that the pain is a lie.

SOFI (*thinking*). The pain is a lie.
You know I always feel like I'm lying when I say I'm in pain.

EILEEN. Not that you're lying but that the pain is an error. Paul called it the carnal mind.
The belief in matter and not spirit.
And so we have to resist pain because resisting pain is resisting what isn't true. The only true thing is the Infinite Idea, forever repeating itself.

SOFI. Huh.

EILEEN. I'm not saying I believe this anymore but I'm not saying I *don't* believe it anymore.

SOFI. Right.

She thinks about this for a while.

Eileen that makes me feel awful.

EILEEN. I'm sorry.

SOFI. If pain doesn't mean anything then it's so fucking boring. But if it means what you're telling me, or if it... I guess if it means anything at all then I don't know if I can bear it.

Pause.

I also really do feel like if I had a week in a hotel room with that man in the silk pants we would cure each other. I'm sorry if this is inappropriate.

EILEEN. It's fine.

SOFI. I really have this profound sense that he could fuck the pain out of me. That someone needs to fuck the pain out of me. (*Pause.*)
You know I've been with – I've been with Pete since I was twenty-four?

EILEEN. Mmm.

SOFI. And so when I think I'm being punished sometimes I think I'm being punished for betraying him but other times I think I'm being punished for not betraying him more completely.

Pause.

EILEEN. So talk me through it.
You rent a hotel room – where.

SOFI. Um. Maybe Rome.

EILEEN. Okay you rent a hotel room in Rome and you spend a week together and then at the end of that week what happens? No more pain?

Pause.

SOFI. I guess I picture – okay it's the end of the week and we're lying on the white sheets together and I'm totally spent like there's nothing left inside of me and um… yes. I keep picturing lying there naked and his hand on my hair and the sun through the window.

EILEEN. His hand on your hair.
What does that feel like?

SOFI. Like a warm compress. And we're not in love. It's just physical.
It's just carnal mind.
We're just two naked sleeping bodies.

Pause.

EILEEN. Is it enough to just imagine it?

SOFI.…No.

EILEEN. Try it.
Imagine that it's all already happened. He's already… Close your eyes.

SOFI *closes her eyes.*

So you're here in the hotel room and the week has passed and he has… what did you say exactly? – he's fucked the pain out of you?

SOFI. Yeah.

EILEEN. He's fucked the pain out of you and all is peace. And look.
A warm hand on your hair.

EILEEN reaches out and puts her hand gently on SOFI's head. SOFI's eyes remain closed. If she lets herself tear up in this moment, it is the first time she has allowed herself to do this in front of anyone except her husband in a very long time. Eventually SOFI's iPhone alarm goes off.

What is that?

SOFI. That's my alarm telling me to call an Uber to the airport in five minutes. Sorry.
I'm really obsessive about flying.

She stands up and fishes her phone out of her backpack. It's a little awkward. She resets the alarm.

I gave myself three more minutes. Where is yours?

EILEEN *is confused.*

Where is your pain exactly?

EILEEN. It's my back and my hips and my shoulder. My left shoulder.

SOFI. Is there anything that helps?

EILEEN. Well this and elevating my legs can help. It's been hard to do here but I try to use the pillows in my room.
At home my husband lifts my feet up in the air for fifteen minutes every night and it's the happiest I am all day.

SOFI. Would you let me do it for you? Before I go?

EILEEN. You don't have to do that.

SOFI. I know but I want to.

EILEEN. It's really fine.

SOFI. I know but will you let me? Just for a minute.

For some reason this is a hard decision. Then EILEEN nods. SOFI bends down and lifts up her feet.

Higher?

EILEEN *nods*.

Higher?

EILEEN *nods*. SOFI *is holding them high in her hands.*

There?

EILEEN *nods*.

That feels good?

EILEEN *nods*.

I could have been doing this for you all week.

They are very still. EILEEN*'s eyes remain closed for the remainder of the play.*
At some point SOFI *sits or kneels on the ground with* EILEEN*'s feet on her shoulders.*

EILEEN. You're forty-fo– how old did you say you were?

SOFI. Forty-seven.

EILEEN. I remember when I was forty-nine I started going through menopause and – I'm not saying this is necessarily what's happening to you – I had the most outlandish desires. I mean it was like I was going through puberty all over again but worse.

SOFI. Really? My mother made it sound like a well drying up.

EILEEN. And I've never even –
I'll be honest with you, sex was never a very big deal to me and I never enjoyed it very much. It's something I've done to make my husband happy and to make children and I could never understand why people were so obsessed with it.
But I remember for about two years after I turned forty-nine things were different. I thought about it all the time.
I was so angry at Don and I wanted to leave him but I also wanted to have sex with him and I also wanted to kill him and I fantasized about every man I saw on the street and some women and I remember one day I even fantasized about our dog.
Never repeat that.

SOFI. I won't.

EILEEN. It was a brief period in my life though. It only lasted about two to three years.
And it was extremely difficult while it was going on, I mean I don't know if I've ever been so unhappy actually, but I was also very alive and now I look back on it and I'm glad it happened.
Though I'm not sure I can tell you why.

After a second, the iPhone alarm goes off again. They look at each other.
End of play.

www.nickhernbooks.co.uk

facebook.com/nickhernbooks

twitter.com/nickhernbooks